Jesus Loves Me

Anna Warner

Illustrated by
Jodie McCallum

ISBN: 978-1-60261-266-2

Printed in China

Jesus Loves Me

Jesus loves me! This I know,

For the Bible tells me so.

Little ones to Him belong;
They are weak, but He is strong.

Yes, Jesus loves me.
Yes, Jesus loves me.

Yes, Jesus loves me.
The Bible tells me so.

Jesus loves me!
This I know,
As He loved
so long ago.

Taking children on His knee,
Saying, "Let them come to Me."

Yes, Jesus loves me.

Yes, Jesus loves me.

Yes, Jesus loves me.
The Bible tells me so.

Jesus loves me still today,
Walking with me on my way.

Wanting
as a friend
to give,

Light and love
to all who live.

Yes, Jesus loves me.
Yes, Jesus loves me.

Yes, Jesus loves me.

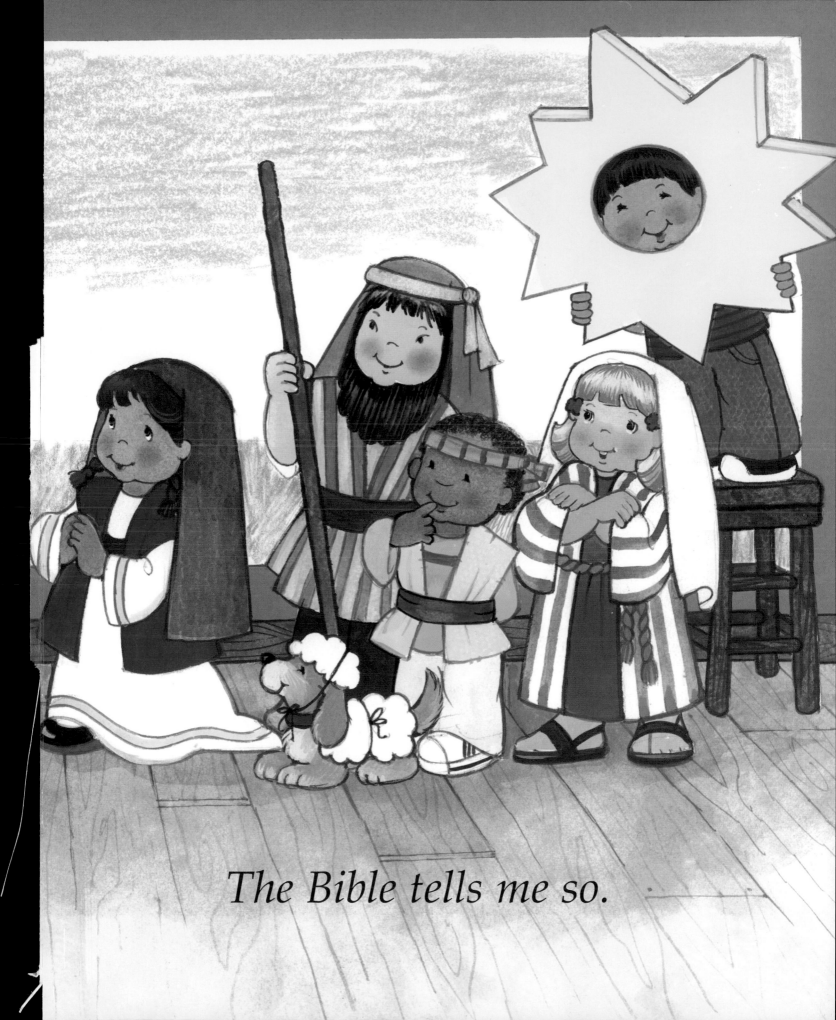

The Bible tells me so.

Jesus loves me! He who cried,
Heaven's gate to open wide.

He will wash away my sin.
Let His little child come in.

Yes, Jesus loves me!
The Bible tells me so.